CW01221434

ANCHOR BOOKS

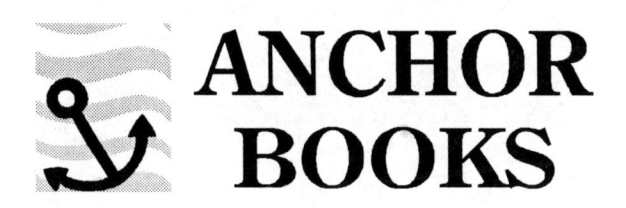

THE ULTIMATE COLLECTION OF TRADITIONAL VERSE 2000

Edited by

Kelly Deacon

First published in Great Britain in 2000 by
ANCHOR BOOKS
Remus House,
Coltsfoot Drive,
Woodston,
Peterborough, PE2 9JX
Telephone (01733) 898102

All Rights Reserved

Copyright Contributors 2000

HB ISBN 1 85930 723 X
SB ISBN 1 85930 728 0

FOREWORD

This special anthology offers a unique collection of poetic expressions and inspirations on life and the world around us. Featuring accessible poems that can be enjoyed and understood by all, we are sure that there is something here for everyone. Each poem communicates across the barriers and helps develop that vital bond between reader and author.

Anyone who ventures within these pages will be treated to a host of delightful and engaging inspirations delivered in earnest from the poetic heart.

Read on and enjoy the unique gift of poetry at its best.

Kelly Deacon
Editor

Contents

Voices At The Water's Edge	Robert J Paget	1
The Eternal Equation	Richard Neve	2
Displacement	Catherine Bradbury	3
The Bomber	Robert John Orr	4
Meditative Musings	Mike Cracknell	5
Ebbtide	John Maginn	6
Fresh Disease	Elliott Nash	7
Fame	Rizwana Yunis	8
Life In A Dream	Sharon Dawn Haines	9
Untitled	Frank Learoyd	10
Food And Drink	J Devine	11
Timothy	Stella Sails	12
A Mother's Plea	Sarah Burke	13
The Message	Estella Garstang	14
The Ice Has Broken	Dennis Rookes	15
Where Did I Go?	Nancy Walecka	16
Wrong Address	Judith A Jinks	17
Alcoholic	Ned Browne	18
From Hannah To Nanna	Harry Mason	19
The Cycle	M A Spencer	20
Tomorrow	Alister	21
The Window	Atia Aslam	22
My Magic Pen	Joyce Sherwood	23
Mother Teresa And Diana	Gus	24
To Love Someone	Jane Stewart	25
Problem Never Ending	Susan Ponter	26
Bradford City	Gabrielle Blakey	27
On Vimy Ridge	Peter Tickner	28
Simple Simon	James Mottram	29
Health	Simon Henry	30
Artificial Reality	Nyima Ryan	31
A 'Ditty' For Christmas	Sue Dawson	32

Untitled	Shirley Phelps	33
Breathe On Me	Mary Turner	34
The Poet And The Painter	Sam Rounce	35
Great Tread And Pulse Of Life	Pamela J Rolinson	36
Scotland	Ian Russell	37
Seasons Come	Hannah Tyler	38
Hillsborough	A E Gilbert	39
Someone Once Told Me I Couldn't Write	A Jowett	40
Eventide	Christopher Stacey	41
Progress	Barbara Sowden	42
Home Coming	Frederick Sowden	43
Full Circle	Mary Prout	44
Do You Understand	Ron Whitehead	45
Language Broadens Our Horizons	J F Jenkins	46
Seeing The Light	Maureen Reid	47
The Funeral	Rhiannon Griffiths	48
A Cry From The Heart	Margaret Yardley	49
Gate Man	Anne R Cooper	50
Conversation With A Giant	Norman Ford	52
Plain English	Hazel Browne	53
Dawn Chorus Bliss	John Reddish	54
UFOs	Bernard Hallas	55
Millennium	Raymond Blakey	56
Angoscia	Louise Rogers	57
He Hated Going To Bed	Joan Wylde	58
Hope And Glory	Kim Montia	59
My Little Tormentor	Marie Kendal	60
Directions	B L Haswell	61
Time Piece	Richard Stoker	62
Hot Soup Tonight!	Tom Ritchie	64
Education . . . What It Ain't	Emmanuel Petrakis	65

Blues	Danny Coleman	66
Tradition	Bert Booley	67
On The M6	Eva L Hewertson	68
Preoccupied	T A Saunders	69
Time (What Time)	Jeremy A Howell	70
They Give All They've Got, And Then Some	Alistair McLean	71
I Wish, For You	Amanda Jackson	72
April Showers	J Hemsley	73
To My Unborn Baby! Boy Or Girl	Michelle Barnes	74
Untitled	John Smurthwaite	75
Good Versus Evil	Gwyneth Rushton	76
Gone Are They	Leslie F Dukes	77
Happy Bank Holiday	Ann Hathaway	78
The Best Is Yet To Be	Betty Mealand	79
Time Humanity Please	Jean Paisley	80
Night After Night	Patricia Cunningham	81
Maytime	Marion Schoeberlein	82
Friends	Poetic M P	83
Paralysed	Don Goodwin	84
I Walked In The Garden	G Poole	85
Childhood Dreams	Jim Sargant	86
My Collie Dog	Keith L Powell	87
Hiding Your Feelings	Samantha Bailie	88
First Past The Post	Glenn Granter	90
Remember	Iris Kruk	91
Internet	Kenneth Mood	92
The Sent Valentine	Roger Thornton	93
No Looking Back	Colin Allsop	94
Irrefutable Image	Ruth Daviat	95
Sandy Bridge	Robert D Shooter	96
Spirituality And Sensuality	K K Kempt	97
Weston-Super-Nowhere	Ian Barton	98

A Female Demand	C Thornton	99
Oh Mother Of Mine	Gary Bullock	100
A Day In The Park	Clare Smith	101
Natural Tones	Burlabh Singh	102
Imagine	Robert Thompson	103
The Fury Of The Sea	Ann Beard	104
Everyday's Extinction	Alan Green	105
Knows No Bounds	Barbara Sherlow	106
Empty Fields	Richard Maslen	107
Wounds To Heal	Edwin Page	108
A New World?	Nishani Balendra	109
Changes Of Time, Through Times We Live	Craig Alan Hornby	110
Planet Earth: Don't Destroy It	David J Hall	111

VOICES AT THE WATER'S EDGE

Jewels of stardust play your games amongst the grains of sand
And build your castles 'ere the tides of time
And winds shall raze your land.

O' children of the sea -
Dance through sparkling waves
And make your voices be heard
Above the mighty roar.
Share your laughter with the sad
Feel free to experience and be glad
For these are echoes and calls of simpler days
The cries of gulls, the wind and waves.

Robert J Paget

THE ETERNAL EQUATION
(On seeing Dr Stephen Hawking on the television)

You sit there, head askew
Pebble-eyed behind those glasses,
Silent, in your electric chair.
Face drawn, mind leaping, while
A finger, clicking on a switch,
Computes electronic words
That send out thoughts across the universe,
And beyond, then disappear
Into black holes inside your head,
Reduced to a mathematical formula.

You spark ideas, vaguely grasped,
That circle slowly in my mind,
On that eternal quest
To discover the meaning of creation.
I have to ask: 'Do you see God?
Or is He just another equation?'

Richard Neve

DISPLACEMENT

Tents regiment the fields
side by side, rank and file,
dankly strung together through the mud

Cold and hungry
I don't want to speak of how I got here -
my son full-grown, yet whimpering in my arms
through this parody of thunder and lightning,
while I bury thoughts of a winter
we wouldn't survive

One morning
swimming up from sleep
time slipped
I reached for the canvas flap
ready to fold it back
and run through sand-dunes
to the sea.

Catherine Bradbury

THE BOMBER
(Lest there be any confusion; the bomber breakfasting here is British, his civilian victims German)

As the bomber takes his seat
At the table for to eat
The husband searches for his wife
As the bomber lifts his knife.

As the bomber butters bread
Fires started by him spread
Fires raging through the night
Ruin not his appetite.

As the bomber stirs his tea
Men dodge falling masonry
Ground is probed and tunnels dug
As the bomber lifts his mug.

As the bomber mops his plate
Delayed-actions detonate
Steel through bone and tissue rips
As the bomber wipes his lips.

As the bomber goes to bed
Parties disinter the dead
Bodies, they are piled in heaps
As the bomber soundly sleeps.

Robert John Orr

Meditative Musings

Here is tranquillity, halcyon bliss.
Heaven has nowhere as peaceful as this.
A more restful haven I have never known
Than this sanctuary where I reflect alone.
I am blessed as any millionaire,
Relaxing, at ease, without a care.

Oh what a wonderfully soothing place,
Away from the hustle of the human race.
The pressures of work are left behind
As delightful thoughts drift through my mind,
Reliving fond memories of days gone by,
Remembering where and when and why.

As I languidly scan my magazine
I rejoice that life is so serene.
In this magic seclusion existence is sweet,
Contentment is close to being complete.
While basking in glorious solitude
I wish that nothing could intrude.

'Are you alright or are you ill?
Are you in that toilet still?
You've been over half an hour in there,
And I am beginning to despair.
You've been reading I'll be bound,
Or have you fallen in and drowned?'

Thus ended my moment of contemplation,
As I return from the world of imagination.
I thought it was too good to be true
To be left in peace upon the loo.
This idyllic interlude could not last,
But did it have to end quite so fast?

Mike Cracknell

EBBTIDE

What now? Now that the end is reached?
Only redundant tradewinds now that the boat is beached;
Only the empty cartridge and the poor bird lying still,
With Song, like a hymn to silence,
Congealed on the shattered bill.

What now, when the great Dare's over,
And the bugle sounds 'Retreat'
Can make the dead hopes hover
Over new ones twice as sweet?
What but the final heartbeat
Like the old drum sounding 'Charge!'
Out of this done-for row boat,
Into the Pilot's barge!

John Maginn

FRESH DISEASE

Blue skies are above me, the polluted air is around me,
Green grass lies beneath me, another tree falls before me.

What are we doing, we're dying as we speak,
Helpless equals weak, it is harmony that we seek,
There's no way of knowing, for sure.

So fragile is the shirt, can't shield us from the hurt,
Ignore the words of mama, and that's what kills you,
For sure.

The duvet on my bed is the shelter I needed, to comfort
The tired and shroud my aching head, and maybe I thought,
For a second why not, I'd exist into tomorrow, for sure.

For sure.

To outlive my fresh disease, no pain, no shame, just lie back
And take it, with ease.

Elliott Nash

FAME

I love my name,
I love myself and everyone loves me,
Self centred?
I think not!
I have power,
The will to do what I want
When I want.
I am a rebel with the desire to be rich,
I have the desire to have fame.
My fans running below me
Crying out my name,
Me staring at them in disgust,
Such things are not worth my attention,
But I have to keep them happy,
So I pretend I like them.
The media, begging for interviews,
But my time is precious,
I live in luxury.
All of this is but a dream,
Soon the day will come
When my dreams will become reality,
You can scoff all you want
But I will prove all of you wrong
Let me prove myself to you.
I can show you the stories I write
The mystery that lurks within them,
These best-sellers will make me rich,
And give me my devoted fans.
One day.
That day is not far away.

Rizwana Yunis (14)

LIFE IN A DREAM

Seeing through illusions deep
I lie in bed awaiting sleep
For my life seems like it's just beginning
My eyes start to flicker I'm almost spinning
Every night in a light of my own
This different life is suddenly shown

Oh, what will it be tonight?
About my favourite time in flight
Or the time I lost my way
Or of a child full of play
Or the time we sat down bored
Possibly the time our heroes scored

What seemed so long
And always strong
Had to start to fade
Just like every spot of shade
As those eyes start to flicker
Voices of people start to bicker
I now lie in a room on my own
I never fear life's unknown

Sharon Dawn Haines

UNTITLED

A field of flowers, some sweet, some wild
Some die off without a smile
But those that stay the summer long
Give joy to us that walk among the grasses and hills
Before the winter brings the chills
Oh! Happy summer days of youth
When hopes were high and all was truth
All the boys and girls with smiles
You could with joy walk on for miles
Maybe now that I am old
A child will smile and stop the cold

Frank Learoyd

FOOD AND DRINK

Apple pies that reach your eyes,
  Cakes and buns to fill your tums,
    Puds and sweets, all good treats,
      Spicy breads all topped with seeds,
        Soups and herbs like tiny weeds,
      Meat and juicy steaks,
        Coffee and cream for those tiny breaks.

Fish and chips with creamy dips,
  Lemons and oranges with tarty pips,
    Pickles and chutney fruity and nice,
      Gin and tonic topped with ice,
        Stew and dumps with meaty lumps,
      Shepherds cottage pie,
        Give us more, we cry!

Strawberries and cream, what a delight,
  For the last caramel we all fight,
    Ices, all colours, oh! so bright,
      Omelettes so fluffy and light,
        Oh! Let there be another bite.

Chocolates and creams and other delights,
  Salads, full of juicy tomatoes, lettuce, cucumbers - bright,

Wine, dark sweet and fine,
  Sparkling and dry, straight from the Rhine,
    Champagne to raise the toast,
      Sherry to greet your host,
        Ginger, orange, pineapple juice,
      Oh! Please let me loose,
        At all that food and drink!

J Devine

Timothy

'The car's outside,' I heard him say, 'what's your plans 'Sir' for today?'
My thoughts were winging back nigh, to the little boy that did not cry.
The blitz was on, the forties saga, not much joy and not much laughter.
My bedroom was the kitchen floor, my bed, a sack, placed
                                                near the door.
My mother had left quietly in the night, while Dad was drinking,
                                                out of sight.
Gran would browse, sitting in the grate, drinking gin, not
                                                thinking straight.
Now and again she'd remember me and put an aspirin in my tea.
The welfare state was not around, the little there was, authority bound.
With tattered clothes and belly not full, I would wander off to school.
The master said a prayer you see, for children with far less than we.
The response was loud, the message clear, it was Timothy's voice,
                                                the loudest here.
I worked so hard and years went by, ambition focused to the sky.
My thoughts disturbed, success today, from rags to riches all the way.

Stella Sails

A Mother's Plea

Another morning full of shame
Please, someone help me stop the pain
I search for my needle to inject my vein
Please God help me, I must be insane.

The children sit at the breakfast table
Baby John still in his cradle
They look with anguish, am I able?
To feed them, the mother with the drug addict label.

What am I doing to these kids of mine?
They have done nothing wrong, as they sit in a line
When the food's placed down, their little eyes shine
For this morning they know that Mummy is fine.

But tomorrow, is a different day
No food in the cupboard and I'll have to say
Sorry kids but you won't eat today
My drug supplier needs his pay.

My children look with fear in their eyes
I'm far too drugged to hear their cries
Too far gone to feel the shame
Please help me stop my children's pain.

A year has passed and I feel fine
That's why I was able to write this rhyme
My children are smiling and I have no shame
I got help and now have no pain.

It's gruelling and hard but it can be done
And now our life is full of fun
Never again will I see them in pain
Drug free life is now my gain.

Sarah Burke

THE MESSAGE

Please send a message to where my daddy's gone,
I'm sure he didn't mean to stay away so long.
Tell him that we love him and miss him every day,
Mummy's looking very sad since he went away.
Tell me where is heaven, is it very far?
I only know that Daddy went there in his car.

Mummy took me in my pushchair to the shop along the street,
As we gazed into the window I heard the sound of feet.
I saw someone in jeans like Daddy used to wear,
And thinking it was him I twisted in my chair
To get a better look as he hurried by.
I even called out to him, but he did not hear my cry.

I know I've seen him on TV no matter what you think,
Sometimes he smiles, he once gave me a wink.
I shouted Daddy! Daddy! And Mummy ran to see,
I thought she would be happy to see what I could see.

Now I am vexed with Mummy, she didn't take a proper look.
I just want my Daddy, not my toys or picture book.
I'm not happy anymore, I don't want to eat,
Even when Mummy makes me a special treat.
I shut my mouth very tight and shake my head about,
When she tries to feed me, I just spit it out.

Estella Garstang

THE ICE HAS BROKEN

You once had a heart of ice
in which your soul follows
the icy heart,
until love struck you down
the warmth you felt in your heart.

You wanted to hold forever
and the smell of sweet roses
set in your heart, breaking you
free from the icy heart.
The ice has broken, setting you
free and now you have love
in your heart.

Dennis Rookes (15)

WHERE DID I GO?

Where did I go?
I say to myself
As I look in the mirror
On the bathroom shelf.
I've got bags under my eyes
They're down to my knees
And everything wobbles when
I have to sneeze!
Policeman look younger
As if they're still at school
And it's chocolate not hunks
That makes me drool!
I used to spend hours
Upon my wild horse
Now I ride on a bus
The steps are so steep of course!
My teeth are a problem
They keep falling out
I have to be careful
If I want to shout!
It's not a lot of fun
When you're getting old
If I was in an auction
I wouldn't get sold!
Mind you, despite getting old
There are a few perks
I don't get hassled
By men who are berks!
I do what I like and people are kind
They just think I'm going out of my mind!

Nancy Walecka

WRONG ADDRESS

It sits there on the table
like a slow-release photoflash,
the morning-after love letter,
flap up, in the last
of my best, lined envelopes,
taken while I slept.
Coffee first, savoured,
sip by sip,
then a dextrous flip,
opening with one hand.
There's nothing there,
turn it over.
Stark words on the back,
where the address should be:
'We're all out of cereal and I'll probably be late.'
Written thoughtfully in pencil,
so I can rub it out
and use the envelope again!

Judith A Jinks

ALCOHOLIC

A lonely candle flickers in the corner of an empty room.
Once it shone brightly,
and filled the room with joy.
But now it battles hopelessly,
choked by its molten wax,
and eaten by its flame . . .
destroyed by what was once its lifeblood.

And just before it becomes but a wisp of smoke,
it turns blue.
Battling to survive.
Desperate to live . . .
craving oxygen.
It fights and fights,
although it knows it's a fight it can't win.

That candle was my friend.

Ned Browne

FROM HANNAH TO NANNA

There was a young maiden called Hannah,
Who was making a fruit cake for her nanna,
When she muttered, 'Oh yuts! Mum's gone and bought the
wrong nuts!'
So I will now have to put them all in the cake - with a spanner!

There was an old lady called Nanna,
Who ate the fruit cake made by Hannah,
Now it beggars belief, for she broke all her 'teef'
And what she said - was in an unladylike manner!

Harry Mason

The Cycle

In the beginning, long ago
dark and empty, silent flow.
A thought, a word, a blinding light,
fiery trails, through boundless night

Expand, extend, begin, create,
make once again, what was of late.
Condense, contract, collect and cool,
spin, sub-divide and make the rule.

Order, position, complicate,
gas, liquid, solid, agitate.
Time lumbers on, the muds to crawl,
the spiral staircase conquers all.

Comprehension slowly dawns,
of all around him that conforms;
to some strange order, all things bow.
He seeks a name, what, why and how?

He makes complex technology,
to probe, to listen, seek and see.
Still others seek inside the depths,
of mind and soul, inner concepts.

Now far out in the distant worlds,
they seek the knowledge, which unfurls.
Plunging the depths of inner space,
admire the micros startling pace.

As space runs out of time at last,
and matter, through one point, is passed.
All that is left of life remain,
to code the message once again.

M A Spencer

TOMORROW

Tomorrow - tomorrow
The day we won't see
There is never tomorrow
Yet tomorrow will be
Tomorrow we wake up
And find it's the same
Tomorrow, there is tomorrow
A mind-boggling game.

Control is the answer
Of tomorrow - 'Refrain'
Don't say tomorrow
By itself in this game
Date it on calendar
Or call it by name
Then peace of mind follows
And again you'll feel sane.

Alister

THE WINDOW

What do you see when you look through the window?
I can see the birds and flowers and trees.
What do you see when you look through the window?
I can see the branches swaying in the breeze.
What do you see when you look through the window?
I can see the children playing outside.
What do you see when you look through the window?
Someone on a bike, going for a ride.
What do you see when you look through the window?
Tell me, tell me, please tell me, do
About what you can see when you look through the window
The only one who can tell me is you.

Atia Aslam

MY MAGIC PEN

I like to write about the beautiful things I have seen
My pen flows and flows over pages bring them all aglow
The wildlife seems to step out of the leaves
And I can almost hear the rustling of the trees
The gentle breeze fans my hand and caress my face
Making my heart beat at a fast pace
The rivers with their beauty as cool as ice and trickling sound
And way up high in the sky a rainbow leads to paradise
The meadows with blades of grass in apple green and
The honey-coloured sunlight comes tumbling down making them gleam
Where lovers walk hand in hand and do dream
At long last I lay my magic pen to rest.

Joyce Sherwood

MOTHER TERESA AND DIANA

The world has lost two good souls,
both looking for their ultimate goals.
To help the suffering and the poor,
starving babies will cry, with swollen bellies for sure.
Caring Lady Di with her glamorous looks,
timeless Mother Teresa in all history books.

On the eve of Diana's funeral day,
old Mother Teresa just passed away.
Diana's gone, tragically lost in her prime,
Old Mother Teresa was ill for some time.

Two humanitarians that really cared,
the world's sorrow truly shared.
So Teresa, teacher of the world and mother of mine,
please send down another pupil from your heavenly shrine.

Gus

TO LOVE SOMEONE

A boy is a word with feelings so true
that's why I'm glad I've met someone like you,
you say all the right things,
you bring sunshine in all that life brings,
so just say the things I long to hear,
because you know darling I'll always be near.
Love is something that comes and goes,
but whether it's true love nobody knows,
because love is something that hurts inside,
but hiding your true feelings is just one big lie.
Love is shared by just two people,
but by hurting a loved one is so, so evil.
So I'm gonna share my thoughts with you,
because you know it's only sweet dreams that come true,
I'm gonna take my time to say,
that my precious love will always stay,
I've told you once and I've told you twice
that to touch your stone-cold heart
would be like breaking your heart of ice.

Jane Stewart

PROBLEM NEVER ENDING

Is there an end to this situation?
A simple process full of complications
All possible solutions comes to dead end
Leaves my heart yearning out for a friend.

A friend to listen, be there, hold my hand
Be kind, considerate and understand
This whole situation leaves me feeling so low
With the whole process travelling very slow.

If I could see the problem, shed some light
The end of the tunnel would be in sight
A problem solved, simply melt away
Would give me strength to face another day.

But no that's not to be
Struggle, hopelessness is all I see
The situation never ending
When all I require is befriending.

To sum up, wind up, sort out
Problem solved without a doubt
How, why, what, got you in this mess,
You were only trying to do your best.

But that's not good enough you see
So go away and let things be
To sort this out an impossible task
But still I hope it will happen fast.

To lift the boxes I would happily do
If that's what's required to get me through
But how can this be
When strength fails me?
Is there a way to set me free?
I was not wanting all this you see.

Susan Ponter

BRADFORD CITY

B radford City are the best
R eally trying to best the rest,
A lways striving to get to the top
D riving their team-mates they never stop.
F orever encouraging to carry on going.
O ver-coming those obstacles to
R each the sky.
D reaming of reaching their goals.

C ongratulating each other on their results
I deas of celebrating begin to form.
T hen back to work
Y et again.

Gabrielle Blakey (14)

ON VIMY RIDGE

The students came by coach to Vimy Ridge
That miserable cold wet misty day
And walked out to the still white monument
Which marks the ending of so many lives
In savage, useless, battle with a foe
Who, fresh faced, eager, were as young as they.
The students, laughing, taking photographs,
Climbing the steps and surveying the view,
Seemed heedless of the sadness all around,
Their carelessness the privilege of youth.
Others, seeming thoughtful and reflective,
May just have been affected by the cold.
I, with shock, stood in that field of battle
Heard, not laughter but the echoing guns.
Boys, recruited from school's year eleven,
As soldiers with their elders from year twelve
Joined the bloody conflict and death's curtain
Urged on by the young bandsmen from year ten.
I shivered, cursed the cold and turned away,
Seeking the warmth of company and coach.
Later, drowsing through the teacher's roll call,
I wished the battle'd ended like that day
So all who'd come to Vimy Ridge went home.

Peter Tickner

SIMPLE SIMON

All the cows were black and white:
Not one of them was blue.
They didn't seem to mind a bit,
But just went moo.

All the pigs were grunting
In and out the sty.
They rolled and wallowed in the mud:
Not one of them could fly.

All the ducks had two legs:
Not one of them had four.
They seemed to be content with two,
Not wanting any more.

All the sheep were bleating:
That's all they ever do.
Not one of them could grunt or quack:
Not one of them could moo.

The horses from the stables
In line came trotting by.
Each one had a stable;
Not one of them a sty.

The rooster, from the haystack,
Cries 'Cock-a-doodle-doo'
He must be puzzled, so am I;
And so, I hope, are you.

James Mottram

HEALTH

He sat there, certain he was going to have a heart attack
Then he burped and the chest pain vanished.

He was convinced he was suffering from stomach cancer
When his tummy felt a little queasy.
But then his bowels moved - and so did the pain.

An ache in his left arm was another portent
Of cardiac arrest,
Until he realised he'd banged it against a shelf that very morning.

Headache was a brain tumour
That turned out to be a hangover.

When he was knocked down by a bus,
The coroner's initial prognosis
Of instantaneous death from multiple injuries,
Was not reversed upon subsequent examination.

Simon Henry

Artificial Reality

I am AR
I am a computer simulation.
I am a figment of your imagination.
You can touch me.
But I am not real.
I am artificial reality.
I am forever or for the moment.
I am AR.

Nyima Ryan

A 'DITTY' FOR CHRISTMAS

Christmas greetings are coming your way
And thoughts turning to gifts for Christmas day
What to get and where to shop
The choice must be good and not cost a lot
Every year we go through this ordeal
Then of course there's the Christmas meal
The turkey to order, the cake to make
The pudding to mix and mince pies to bake
Buying the wine, make sure there's enough beer
Because everyone will want plenty of cheer!
Christmas Eve arrives, what's not done - well tough
Though of course, as ever, there'll be more than enough
The children are excited and you're feeling quite merry
As for Santa they leave a mince pie and a sherry
Christmas day dawns, the kids are up with the lark
As they open their presents, outside it's still dark!
At the end of the day you sink exhausted into bed
Everyone's happy 'cos they've been watered and fed
You feel quite content, then suddenly jump up in fear
As you realise you'll have to do it all again next year!

Sue Dawson

UNTITLED

Could it be too much to ask,
To set aside this one last task,
To shed the layers of despair,
And find the joy that's waiting there.

Can hurt and pain destroy so much,
That love cannot be felt as such,
The shock of grief and sheer dismay,
Dulling the sun on God's bright day.

For waiting, eager in the wings,
A little bird defiant sings,
Just lift your heart up to the sky,
Come on, just do it, you can fly,
But believe it lady, you must try.

Shirley Phelps

BREATHE ON ME

Lord fill me with your holy spirit
Breathe on me
Blow the wind that slowly rages
Safe out to the sea
Let the ocean beds be still
With fish for men to catch
Lead the lost sheep to the shepherd
Safely home at last.

Let not the mountains spit with anger
Peace be with you say
Don't look back because tomorrow
Is another day
Follow now the road to Jesus
Walk in righteousness
He will lead you to the father
Mighty God eternal rest.

Mary Turner

THE POET AND THE PAINTER

The poet and the painter
Went for a walk one day.
The poet said, 'I hear the lark
And smell the new mown hay.'

The painter said, 'I see the hills,
The Malverns mauve and grey
And there's the Severn silver bright.
Oh what a lovely day!'

'It is a lovely day indeed,'
The poet then opined.
'And don't you find the cooling breeze
Blows cobwebs from your mind?'

They wandered on a little way
Down by a chuckling brook.
They had no path to follow
'Cept where their fancy took.

They came upon a garden
Beside a charming villa.
The poet cried, 'Oh what's that scent?
Oh yes. Of course, vanilla.'

The artist scanned the borders
Full of flowers he knew.
'I'm sure it's from the heliotrope
And such a lovely blue.'

Between them they missed ne'er a thing,
Though she had lost her sight
And he was blind, they still enjoyed
The priceless gift of life.

Sam Rounce

GREAT TREAD AND PULSE OF LIFE

Great tread and pulse of life
its boisterous exuberance
vivid sound
intense, ongoing, spinning, leaping, twisting,
plunging, ascending.
Descending down avenues of tower blocks
and ear-searing traffic.
Internet, computer, e-mail, mobile phone -
pinstripe suit and polished shoe
arms held high in stock market -
meetings, agendas, a bus to catch
rushing, crashing, shouting, chaos!
Voice, nerve, heart-pounding, no time to wait.
Eating fast food - an hour in the gym -
bursting through ticket barriers
whistle piercing
to catch the last train out.
Midnight day ending - dreaming, tossing,
hallucinations -
deep sleep too late.
Alarm ringing, screaming.
Great tread and pulse of life - its boisterous
exuberance - vivid sound - begins again.

Pamela J Rolinson

SCOTLAND

Scotland is a nation
Which we talk about with pride
And recall our great achievements
Such as ships built on the Clyde

Our Harris tweed and whisky
Are renowned in every land
Our rivers and our mountains
The scenery so grand

The Scottish hospitality
Is praised both far and wide
And thousands flock to visit us
To see our countryside

We welcome them with open hearts
And make them glad they came
To see our glorious scenery
Our wildlife and our game

Our land is steeped in history
And our architecture's grand
I wonder how we pack so much
Into such a compact land

So when you are wondering where to go
To spend your well-earned rest
Just make your way to Scotland
And you'll agree it is the best

Ian Russell

SEASONS COME

Seasons come and seasons go
Pick up our bags and off we all go.
We start the year all merry and bright
Not a care or worry have we in sight.
But as the months come to an end
Then off we all go and leave our friends.
Christmas comes with style and grace
Send out cards to various place.
We wish every one good health, good cheer,
As we wait for the following year.
We raise our glasses, we say all the best,
Good luck, good health to all of the rest.

Hannah Tyler

HILLSBOROUGH

Just a day out to watch the game
Doesn't seem much to ask
But by the time that I got home
So much had come to pass
The bodies lay upon the ground
Surrounded by a fence
Just a day to watch the match
It doesn't make much sense
I was one who walked away
I walked away unharmed
But quite a few supporters
Never will go home
But still I like to think
That my brother who was seven
Is watching angels play the game
In a stadium called heaven.

A E Gilbert

SOMEONE ONCE TOLD ME I COULDN'T WRITE
(For Laura)

Someone once told me I couldn't write,
And quite willingly I believed.
Little did I realise
They had me totally deceived.

This cuts deep, very deep,
Wounds which may never heal.
Worlds crashed to the ground,
Despair I began to feel.

My dream had been shattered,
Until I told a friend
Who realised my dilemma
And assured me it's not the end.

So now I write this poem,
As you can clearly see,
I do this for myself,
That's all that matters to me.

I'll use my writing talent,
And will do come what may.
Those comments bother me no more,
I don't care what they say.

A Jowett

EVENTIDE

Day has ended, shadows falling
Now twilight dew
Settles on green meadows
Moon is rising too.
Darkness like a velvet cloak
Over all descends
Church bells softly ringing
New enchantment lend.
High above the countryside
Fields frosty white
Wild geese are winging
Through the starry night
Eerie cry of ghosting owl
Rabbits in the copse
Fleeing to their burrow
From a prowling fox
Moon growing dimmer
Stars very few
Eastward sky tinted with a rosy hue.
Morning mist disappearing
As a radiant sun
Ascends into the heavens
New day has begun.

Christopher Stacey

PROGRESS

Stagnant and muddy lies the water,
In a once crystal clear village pond,
No more wide open spaces for children to play,
In the fields and woods beyond.

Developers built on this pleasant land,
Factories and housing estates,
Trade effluent seeps via the beck to the pond,
Destroying natural life form in its wake.

The factories emit obnoxious smells,
Polluting our clean country air,
Wild flowers and hedgerows have disappeared,
Replaced by tarmac roads cold and bare.

This modern day environment named progress,
Should benefit all mankind,
Providing employment and housing,
But what simple pleasures have we left behind.

Barbara Sowden

HOME COMING

After thirty years I paid a visit,
Back to the village where I was born,
I had been missing it for a long time,
Became homesick and so forlorn.

My sister welcomed me with open arms,
And said there's a surprise in store,
The village is so much changed,
You won't know it anymore.

We walked up through the village,
The duck pond had been filled in,
In its place a tarmac mini roundabout,
To me that was a sin,

On the village green were bungalows,
Gone was the market square,
Tarmaced it was with painted white lines,
Five pounds to park a car there,

That's not all my sister laughed,
The post office, and the little chip shop,
Mr Jones the bakers, Mr Clegg the butchers,
Now gone all been given the chop.

The wood where we gathered bluebells,
That now is a housing estate,
Motorway came through the village,
That sealed the cricket field's fate.

Strangers now fill the village,
Many of those you knew died or moved away,
Houses here are at such a premium,
The young could not afford to stay,
Soon I fly back to Australia,
I am so sick of home I can't wait for the day.

Frederick Sowden

Full Circle

Trudge on bitter beat of winter wind,
Moan from behind a frantic symphony.
Then leave as spring's vision
Urges in summer's languid garden.
Her fragrant blooms bow to autumn's glory
Until her time-spent leaves return
To comfort Earth's chilly bosom
In her long and promising winter sleep.

Mary Prout

DO YOU UNDERSTAND

When the evening returns just like a friend.
When the night comes to set me free.
When the quiet hour beyond the day
Makes peaceful sounds within me,
I take a drink from a glass of old wine,
Then close my eyes and I could make it real,
And feel it real, just one more time,
Just one more time!
Can you hear it there, can you hear it?
From another time, another by-gone place,
Do you remember it, too?
When we lay in our warm bed,
Listening to songs we loved to sing.
But it's hard to remember now,
From another time, another by-gone place.
We gave them all away, all away,
Like marbles in the school playground.
Memories and dreams of a lovely time.
Do you know what I mean?
Do you really understand what I mean?

Ron Whitehead

LANGUAGE BROADENS OUR HORIZONS

Think if we had to do business by sign messages,
what a muddle the world would be in.

Languages is begotten, born and unageing.

English is traced back to ancient Greece
with many similarities of Spanish, Latin and French words.

With such a wide vocabulary
it provides a wonderful balance of words

The word skills of William Shakespeare echoes life and travelling.
In common with most techniques we talk in local dialects.
Regional related languages.

Without a word wavelength
there could be no chemistry between nations.
One thing comes to fore, even the poor beggar
who sits down on the pavement is not lost for words.
It bonds the impediments even if you are educated at Eton.
Do I make myself clear?

J F Jenkins

SEEING THE LIGHT

On a night out I caught your eye
I do believe it was in a pub called 'The Lay-by'
You took your time to say 'hello'
You need not had bothered as you were only out for show
If that was all you wanted
You should have made that clear from the start -
Saved me the trouble of nursing my broken heart!
As time has passed by, I no longer think of you
I have cried all my tears that I intended to do
I know now I have buried all my pain
Finally got rid of you from my brain
My life now has changed in such a way
I awake every morning fresh to start a new day
My zest for life, has shown me that I do
Not need to conform and become a wife - at
Least not at this moment in time, after all I am in my prime.
I have a lot of statements still to make
It's do it now 'girl' make or break.

Maureen Reid

THE FUNERAL

Black-garbed figures scattered among gravestones -
Moss green and leaning with age,
Disjointed notes of the hymn tune,
The minister's funeral face.

Crow and jackdaw, jet-black above,
Adding cacophonous sounds,
But the blackbird sings,
Unaware of all around.

The broken-hearted and uncaring
In controlled silence unite.
The hope of a better hereafter,
And that God will decide to be kind.

The crow and jackdaw fly away,
The blackbird sings elsewhere.

Trestled tables with starched white cloths,
Bread and butter, cheese in small cubes,
Madeira and fruitcake, the steaming urn -
A funeral tea in the vestry.
The *crescendo* of mourners' voices
Greet, recollect and pretend
That they're a family together,
And life doesn't come to an end.

The crow and jackdaw return,
The blackbird sings again.

Rhiannon Griffiths

A Cry From The Heart

I am a helpless refugee,
But it's not what I want to be.
I need your help to survive,
I desperately want to stay alive.

Save us from this dark despair,
Show us that you really care,
Anything that you can give,
Gives us hope, and a chance to live.

I lost my home and family too,
But what was I supposed to do,
Faced with the barrel of a gun,
What was left, but to turn and run?

But one day soon I will return,
Those responsible will a lesson learn,
So stand by us in this time of sorrow,
And give us hope for a new tomorrow.

Margaret Yardley

GATE MAN

The creation of the world in its natural state
Was a gift from the heavens
And the good shepherd keeps watch by the strong wooden gate

He watches with concern at the destruction done
By the hateful that's so thoughtless with their tongue
He sees the earth with its luscious green grass
He sees the high lands and the water winding through
                                      the very blood of our land

Conditions in some parts of the world are very poor
The hideous heat and the dry ground and hunger around
Some people there still want to fight
Have they a conscience, not to help and cause the loss of life
How can the heart of this man at the gate
Bear the pain that sends the spear hame
And we are shown-up by a mere animal that passes by tame

In this western world, cruelty has all forms
And can often leave our heart battered and torn
Yes people get out of hand and cruelty is the decease of our land
As they destroy by tongue action and deed
And the soul of the perpetrator this great man can read
Then sometimes it isn't what is said and done
It is the sheer neglect and absolute nothingness
That did the same rot as the gun
Oh see to ourselves and take a big slice of the cake
And we'll simply neglect and leave the starving and wounded
                                        at the gate
To know the person that's blessed by just enough to get by
You could be certain that person would hear my cry

Yes care knows pain and in blindness we'll finally rest in our hame
And when the one who makes the final comment speaks
Into our hearts it will reach and we'll know we are hame
Because that person will simply say 'This casualty was sane.'

Anne R Cooper

CONVERSATION WITH A GIANT

We thank you for ringing. The complaint that you're bringing
Is a genuine one I can see,
But the expert it needs is now based up in Leeds.
You should really have pressed button 3.

But if you find button 3 fails, just give me your details;
I'll get back to you soon, never fear.
Sit back and relax, while I seek out the facts,
And I'll phone you today . . . or next year.

If you press button 2, you will find you are through
To our agent in East Pakistan,
Who knows nothing at all of things west of Nepal.
He can't help, but knows someone who can.

What, you're keen on conversing with a real living person?
Then it's no use your holding the line.
I'm afraid you've no choice, all you get is my voice,
And I'm based in Newcastle-on-Tyne.

You may find someone live if you press button 5,
Though you could have a bit of a wait.
For our man at that station's just gone on vacation
So try pressing 7, or 8.

Though your phone bill has soared, you can now rest assured,
That we're human, whatever folk say.
We did not leave you cold, we just put you on 'hold'
And played Brahm's Concerto in A.

So please don't be nervous, we are here at your service.
We wish only to make your life better.
And if all is not well, simply give us a bell -
Or maybe it's quicker by letter!

Norman Ford

PLAIN ENGLISH

My teacher said to me 'You must not use 'nice'
It's not a 'nice' word you see,
It doesn't mean anything.'

When I walked it was invigorating, sharp, long,
Or slippery on the ice.
But not nice.

I had a 'nice' dinner, but no, not nice!
It was tasty, sustaining, filling,
Healthy with salad, or with grilling,
But not nice.
Another word must suffice.

I had a new dress, it was 'nice'
But no! Not nice!
It was long, it was frilly
It was blue.
It fitted me well.
It was a hefty price, and I loved it
But it was not nice!
No! No! It was not nice.
So how can I tell my best friend about it?
'Oh Miss! Go to hell!'
It was nice!

Hazel Browne

DAWN CHORUS BLISS

Sitting on the very lovely seat,
Near the pond in Northcliffe woods,
Sky getting lighter,
Birds awake.

Dawn of so much beauty,
Tranquil freshness,
Magic in the air,
April morning, life be very daring.

No wind, nature's lightest touch,
Pond of reflection,
Water of wonder and mystery,
Bliss perfect closeness.

John Reddish

UFOs

Somewhere deep in the velvet void
The UFOs cruise around,
Hiding behind the scudding clouds
Determined not to be found.

A fleeting glimpse of flickering light
A hint of vapour trail,
Disguising themselves as a shooting star
Or a Comet without a tail.

They hover at night over country lanes
When the countryside is asleep,
Observed by the lonely traveller
And the ever present sheep.

Are they stocking their larders
Even aliens we suppose must eat,
Or, are they seeking contact
Perhaps one day we shall meet.

And come that day, we shall realise
As their minds control our will,
That we, the denizens of Earth
Have merely been standing still.

Bernard Hallas

MILLENNIUM

Since man evolved in this ancient world
Three thousand, thousand years have gone
Mostly unnoticed, unrecorded
So what's so different about this particular one?

There'll still be wars, disease and death
We'll still be asking why oh why
We cannot use for the common good
Our vast technological array.

Instead of pitting man 'gainst man
With further precious resource lost
For when mankind will have to unite
Will we in time compute the cost?

Yet the human race is a great success
Six billion of us now, then seven, then ten
Consuming, polluting, warming the globe
But not forever. What happens then?

Beneath our feet, whether rock or melt
Untouched and unchanged by sun, wind or rain
Ninety-nine percent of this planet Earth
Yields not a gram to the vital food chain.

Doctors may decide who lives or dies
Bad enough - yet perish the thought
Some faceless commission may give us
Permission to be even born or not.

The steepening curve to self-destruct
Questions whether thinking man, Homo Sapiens
Will face the dreaded real issue
Can we exist even one more millennium?

Raymond Blakey

ANGOSCIA

Tomorrow she may awaken . . . or not awaken.
A new day dawn . . . her next or the last to be?
It is her husband who had not awakened.

What fate brings here this silent watcher
to a high place facing ruins of antiquity?
Tomorrow she may awaken . . . or not awaken.

Morn may reveal a glow betokening
the mystical rising of the sun for all to see.
It is her husband who had not awakened.

Now the boats of Catalunyan fishermen
leave harbour, sail seemingly into infinity.
Tomorrow she may awaken . . . or not awaken.

Why so fearful that she is forsaken,
her anxious thoughts presage fatality?
It is her husband who had not awakened.

Returned home she may wait, expectant,
for one she never more will see.
Tomorrow she may awaken . . . or not awaken.
It is her husband who had not awakened.

Louise Rogers

HE HATED GOING TO BED

There was a peculiar young man named Fred
Who really hated going to bed
When asked why this was
He said 'It's because
It's nearer to getting up!' he said

Joan Wylde

Hope And Glory

Our warriors are always brave
We know they'll stand and fight
We trust them to protect us
And to do the thing that's right

How to kill, their stock in trade
We need not know the facts
Preferring to ignore
That to defend one must attack

We sanitise the butchery
Each cut is swift and clean
A minimalist view ensures
No drop of blood is seen

Our soldiers have the biggest hearts
An army of the best
The enemy is always wrong
And any doubt suppressed.

Kim Montia

MY LITTLE TORMENTOR
(To Mandy with love)

All was quiet
Until I was seven
Until a little bundle came
And changed my life forever
My little tormentor.

Sleepless nights, sharing rooms
Fallouts, fights and laughter,
Never a dull moment in our home
My little tormentor.

There came a time
When things had to change
I grew up
And was never the same
Always a shadow followed me round
From going out with boys
To a night on the town
My little tormentor.

From baby to teenager
And now to adult
No longer a tormentor
But someone to share
All the memories we hold
Of sisters so dear
My little tormentor.

Older and wiser
And moving apart
All growing up to travel far
But never forgetting the love
So deep in our hearts
My little tormentor.

Marie Kendal

DIRECTIONS

Dawning sun-rays greet with golden welcome,
Flickering through the leaves of the waymark tree.
So, Pilgrim, begin your life-quest journey.
Take one last look at the cold blue sea.
Go to the distant snow-peaked mountain.
Fill your lungs with the scent of wild thyme.
Look eastwards cross the fertile valley.
The emerald hill is the one you must climb.
Down to the island of the crystal lake,
See where duck and geese construct their nest.
On to the far off silver birch spinney,
Watch butterflies play whilst you rest.
Continue to the ancient dark oak forest,
Amongst ferns and pimpernels you spend the night.
Badger creeps, hedgehog snorts as you slumber,
Awaiting the sun's welcome light.
Moonbeams dance like flickering fairies,
Dark shows the Dog Star and the Plough.
Night appears in such wondrous splendour.
To its creator, I can only bow.
Towards the headwaters of the whistling river,
The otter shyly watches from bubbling streams,
A creation of some grand plan dreams.
The path by wild honeysuckle is yours,
It leads to where violets and cornflower grow.
Admire the red poppies and purple campions,
Streamlets appear and vanish, where no one knows.
You will see the Temple of All Knowledge,
And breathe the early morning air so clear.
Learn to appreciate all that surrounds you.
Discover why I love Planet Earth so dear.

B L Haswell

TIME PIECE

Where would we be without women?
Where would they be without men?
What would we do in the evening
As the clock on the wall reaches ten?

How will they be in the morning?
How will men manage to wait?
When everyone stays in bed late
As the clock on the wall reaches eight?

He's staying out late 'til the morning:
As he's just met a girl that is new,
Who's told him that she'll be true
As the clock on the wall reaches two?

They walk hand in hand through the smog
Silent thoughts with a look and a nod;
She can't believe 'he's attracted to me'
When the clock on the wall reaches three.

They'd met for a sandwich at lunchtime
Then on to the shops and a tour;
After tea he's expecting more
As the clock on the wall reaches four.

What can they do? Where can they go?
She will ask him to drive
Then visit his dive
As the clock on the dashboard hits five.

They close out the fog with a curtain
Together they're ready to learn;
Wow, he thinks, she knows a few tricks
As the clock on the wall reaches six.

That night she goes to bed early
She reads without taking much in
Her last thought on the stroke of eleven
Is to rise bright and early at seven.

She wakes with a start in the morning
Realising it's ever so late
Standing there stretching and yawning
As the alarm from the clock blares out eight.

On the train to the city
Her decision is witty
She'll ask him to dine
On the last stroke of nine.

Her arrival at work's a bit late,
She's making the tea for them all
As usual and thinks much of men
As the clock on the wall reaches ten.

They're home very late the next morning
The trains and the buses have stopped;
He thinks will they manage some fun
As the clock on the wall chimes out one.

Oh where would we be without women?
And where would we be without men?
What would we do in the morning
As the day starts all over again?

Richard Stoker

HOT SOUP TONIGHT!

Late trees,
Stiff breeze,
Rustle of leaves,
Golden light;
In the park,
Sun's ark,
Turning dark . . .
Stars in sight!

Home we go,
Radio low,
Promise of snow,
'Conditions right!'
Dying sun,
Badger's run,
Day is done . . .
Hot soup tonight!

Tom Ritchie

EDUCATION ... WHAT IT AIN'T

Education isn't maths or geometry
It isn't grammar, trigonometry,
It isn't computers, historical dates,
It isn't statistics or rates.
It isn't chemistry, biology,
Literature or sociology,
It isn't languages, facts,
It's how one is, how one acts:
It isn't sports or logistics,
It isn't tests or statistics,
It isn't rules, an exam,
It's what you are, what I am.
It isn't cramming or books,
It's how your soul really looks,
It's not a Master's Degree,
It's how you really treat me.
It isn't grades or good spelling,
It's your behaviour most telling,
It isn't physics or figures,
But hands on flowers, not triggers.
It isn't science, fine style
That makes living worthwhile,
Do we produce learned fools?
Who teaches wisdom in schools?

Emmanuel Petrakis

BLUES

If you don't want the blues, occupy your mind
Use your senses, leave melancholia behind
Don't give yourself time to become sad
Take up a dozen hobbies, make yourself glad
Glad you don't dwell on the darker side
But imagine, down a rainbow you slide
Landing in a field of magical plants
That cheer you up, can make you dance
Where furry creatures actually talk
And without fear with humans walk
Where there's no sign of any danger
And children needn't fear a stranger
The sun shines bright, there is no cancer
And everyone can be a ballet dancer
Skipping along, in shiny red shoes
Safe in the knowledge the best way
To avoid the blues, is simply not
To read, watch or listen to bad news.

Danny Coleman

TRADITION

An Englishman's home is his castle they say
But the one who owns it can take it away
To build a motorway or office block
This would be the little man's lot

He could stand at his door and rave and shout
But the owner would get a court order to sling him out
A bailiff with a sledge hammer will smash down his castle door
Of his castle there be no more

He may rant and rave and call the owner a dirty name
But the owner just grins and says it is the court to blame
After living in his castle for forty years
He will leave his little home his eyes filled with tears.

Bert Booley

ON THE M6

Speed down the slip-road - can we get in?
In front of that caravan - oh what a din!
Houses, churches - part of the scene.
Why all this rush - what does it mean?
Here comes a bridge - now we've whizzed past.
Into the slow lane - now in the fast.
Weave in and out - now past that lorry.
Can't we go slower - what is the hurry?
Hills, rivers - blend into one.
Look at those colours - blink and they've gone.
Sheep in their hundreds - do they ever stop grazing?
Now there are forests - isn't it amazing?
Did you notice that sign? You've to slow down to 30.
Look at that sports car - isn't it dirty?
Now we are crawling - what a long queue.
I'm getting quite hungry - how about you?
When will we get there - when can we stop?
Ah, here come the services - I'm ready to flop.
Smelly old diesel - and greasy hot fat,
Queues for a cuppa - could have done without that.
Head for the ladies - spotlessly clean,
Proud to be British - fit for a queen.
I'm now feeling better - shall we start off again?
I wonder if next time we should travel by train!

Eva L Hewertson

PREOCCUPIED

Preoccupied
Can't seem to relax
Het up
Thinking about what's bothering me
Got to travel
And I'm awful at geography!
Need to overcome this fear
When I do
Everything will be clear!

T A Saunders

TIME (WHAT TIME)

How often we forget time!
From the hour of birth,
Blink - and it has diminished,
The highest hope of pride and power has flown,
Vanished long ago my strength in youth,
Such is time to destroy the soul
Claiming its right, my life removed,
The cold shadow of age haunts my vision
While I sleep - I reflect on childhood hopes,
But now the sands of time fade in unison with my heart
Too late to save!
I linger in weakness,
Time continues.

Jeremy A Howell

THEY GIVE ALL THEY'VE GOT, AND THEN SOME

My buddies have left me,
left me all on my own,
No call in the morning,
just go on alone.

The journey ain't easy,
no peace for me now,
The Big C was a hard one,
don't try it for fun.

Somebody wanted my tomorrows,
when I'd only got half-done,
And you feel they're kinda precious
getting near to that last one.

So my buddies have left me,
just go on home,
We don't need you no more,
you can do it alone.

Alistair McLean

I Wish, For You
(To Marie)

I'm sorry for all the bad times
You've had
I'm sorry for all the pain
I'm sorry for all the tears
You've cried
I wish I could be there
To wipe every single tear away.

I wish for you I could take
Away the pain
I wish for you I could take
Away the bad times you've had
I wish for you every tear
Would be ones of happiness
I wish for you all the bad times
Would be good.

I'll take away the heartache
I'll take away the pain
I'll take away the tears you've cried
And just leave you with happy days.

I'll make the wishes right here, right now
So keep this poem in your heart
My wishes might come true
Then all you will be left with
Is just simple happy days.

Amanda Jackson

APRIL SHOWERS

Thank Heaven there is rain today
To wash the dust and grime away;
To freshen all the fields and leas
And brighten up the plants and trees.

Without the rain each flower would die -
There would be no rainclouds in the sky.
All nature would be parched and brown,
With odour and filth in every town.

Birds would no longer sing on high,
On glorious rain they all rely.
But beauty will shine on each spring day
When those *April showers* come our way.

J Hemsley

TO MY UNBORN BABY! BOY OR GIRL

A Christmas wish
A dream come true
A new little life so brand-new

A time for smiles, laughter too
Happiness knowing
We have Shannon, now you

Whatever you are, a girl or a boy
Doesn't matter to me
As long as you feel at your best
No need to love you any less

As whether you are a girl or a boy
I know you will bring us loads of joy

Shannon will help me
To look after you
Love and care
From day one right through

She will protect you
And always be there
We'll always be your family
To love and care.

Michelle Barnes

UNTITLED

The question posed,
A silence fell,
I thought inward,
Oh, what the hell!
Why did I ask
That drunken Scot,
Was Glasgow in
Scotland or what?

The bar had cleared
I felt the draught,
The lunatic in me,
Just laughed,
They'd browned me off,
Sometime before,
Supporting Rangers
Evermore
We drowned them out,
With 'Liverpool Lou'
You have to sometimes,
Haven't you?

Nothing happened
Sure enough
They just backed down,
We'd called their bluff
With hindsight
It could have been worse,
Those so-called hard men
Made themselves scarce
It's a decision,
To fight or stay,
Perhaps it's better,
To walk away.

John Smurthwaite

GOOD VERSUS EVIL

Sometimes we feel the dark encroach
  And we feel sure it's not a hoax
Played on us by imagination,
  But we can fight with indignation.
How dare that darkness spoil our mood?
  How dare that fear of dark intrude?
We can fight it with our will,
  By feeling that we surely shall
Not be swamped by evil or despair,
  Nor be swayed by things that are so unfair.
We deserve a share of hope and light,
  We can withstand evil and gladly fight.
The exercise will warm our spirits,
  Then with the glow of effort in us
It should grow easier to find the way
  Lit by these strivings of each day.
Can evil ever withstand
  Concerted effort from an honest hand?
I trust and hope it never can.
  And goodness, really, in the long run,
Is, very simply, much more fun.
  So never let it be thought or said
That we were held in thrall by fear and dread.
  All of that can be overcome
By a force as powerful as the sun
  Which radiates its own pure light
And has ample power to banish night.

Gwyneth Rushton

GONE ARE THEY

Old bricks and mortar, and broken tiles
Scattered around . . . so untidy are the piles
'They; all that once were houses,' just two up . . . two down,
Standing in narrow streets . . . built 'back to back'
With their rows and rows of chimney stacks;
Many were the doors, each house had little windows
Which played a tune, when e'er the wind blew
For they did not fit . . . how they rattled;
They had open yards with white-washed walls,
Against which most of the kids would bounce a ball,
Soon a neighbour would call out 'You lot! Clear off -
I'm washing today . . . so go on, gerroff,'
For across the yard they hung their lines,
On which they hung their sheets . . . and fines;
No washing machines nor launderettes,
Just 'dolly tubs' and 'dolly legs'
Now all that remains are the open spaces,
Gone are they . . . they all had familiar faces.
They were the ones whom sat at their open door,
They'd say hello to whom may pass,
No matter should they be of higher class,
They are no more . . . but they were so friendly,
The houses gone
Now all is empty.

Leslie F Dukes

HAPPY BANK HOLIDAY

Rolling through mountain roads splendid
Rat race behind us, tired minds mended
Hillsides foliaged by tall trees green
Countryside wonders her picturesque scene
We stopped to take in this scenic place
Summer breezes bathed my ashen face
Found a beach where we paddled together
Absorbing every hour of warm summer weather
Warm sandy beach, fresh breezes brush my hair
Polluted city behind us, take in sea salt air
Surrounded by clouds dusted blue speckled grey
Enjoying summer sun's warm bright yellow ray
Collecting pretty seashells, we paddle and splash
Through ocean's cold waters happy children dash
Wonderful day, our souls fortified and restored
Hump our belongings, children and the dog aboard
Wonderful day over, return to dissolution
To busy cities, car jams and polluted confusion
Back to hubble and bubble, that old hum drum way
Return to city after dark on a lovely summer's day

Ann Hathaway

THE BEST IS YET TO BE

At the age of thirty
Came time of reflection,
Began to be thirsty
For self-satisfaction.

Living to convention
Up until that moment,
Not daring to question
If I was quite content.

Sadness was not the source,
A good childhood recall,
But I followed a course
Expected by them all.

At the age of thirty
Knew at last wakefulness,
Consciousness seemed worthy
After total darkness.

By real self confronted,
That inner insistence
Could not remain stunted
Nor tolerate silence.

Upon revelation,
Embarking on my quest
Of life's realisation,
Who I am, the great test.

On discovering myself,
Warm, sensual and earthy,
Old values on the shelf
At the age of thirty.

Betty Mealand

TIME HUMANITY PLEASE

A time revolution came our way,
the people broke their bonds, refused to play.

No clock to look at night and day,
without the weather forecast what will we say.

To eat when hunger pangs are strong,
in light or dark neither being wrong.

Age not having any sway,
you do the job, collect the pay.

Spontaneity everywhere,
things starting up without a care.

Worried people live no more,
we've all forgotten what that's for.

Jesus called and it's alright,
it's like he said, there's no more night.

Past, present, future all combine,
people just live and that is fine.

Jean Paisley

NIGHT AFTER NIGHT

Night after night, alone in the bed,
Desperate for company, for your arms,
To hold, to comfort, to reassure,
To be swept, to be cosseted by your charms.

Your eyes are all I see in the dark,
Your deep voice is all that I hear,
Your skin is all that I touch at night,
Your departure is all that I fear.

Your name is all that I call with my lips,
Your aftershave is all that I can smell,
The beat of your heart is all I can hear,
Then silence, sheer total, utter hell.

The hours spent with you are over,
You're gone, you've found another, I hate,
Don't care how kind, how loving she is,
She stole you, she sealed my fate.

To wake once more, wrapped in your arms,
Is all that I ask, all I dream,
Instead I'm left wondering, scared of the future,
Just left alone, to scream and scream.

Patricia Cunningham

MAYTIME

The sun is a friend
on my back.
Trees are green castles,
flowers lamps
growing in the grass.
While the world
sings of lilacs
my heart lays down
its winter stones.

Marion Schoeberlein

FRIENDS

Side by side we walk each day, no matter what the weather,
He cannot speak but I understand, as we walk along together,
What lovely big brown eyes he has, they sparkle and shine with love
Sometimes we both sit on one chair, giving him a kiss and a hug.

We look into each other's eyes, he looks towards the door,
That's his way of telling me, it's time for a walk once more,
We walked along, I spoke to him, he knew just what I said,
'It's time we went home old boy, for a cup of tea and bed.'

He wagged his tail and gave a whine,
As if to say 'I've known,
That you don't feel so well tonight,
Come on then, let's go home.'

Poetic M P

PARALYSED

Please don't feel sorry for me, because I'm paralysed.
You may think I'm useless, but not in God's eyes.
I am precious and one day He will set me free,
From this wheelchair and the condition that hinders me.
When I walk with Jesus, all paralysis will be gone.
When I go to live with Jesus, nothing can go wrong.

Don Goodwin

I Walked In The Garden

I walked in the garden,
   The garden at evening,
I loitered among
   The darkening hours,
I walked in the garden,
   The garden at evening,
I wandered alone
   By the dew wet flowers.

When I walked in the garden
   The garden at evening
I walked in the warmth
   Left from the day.
When I walked in the garden,
   The garden at evening
I felt all the joy
   Still round me lay.

So I'll walk in the garden,
   The garden at evening
I'll walk in the shadow
   That dims out the light
I'll walk in the garden,
   The garden at evening
I'll then know the peace
   That comes with the night.

G Poole

CHILDHOOD DREAMS

Think back to days of childhood dreams,
Of childhood games and childhood schemes,
Was it all so long ago?
How time has flown, where did it go?
In just the twinkling of an eye,
The world has turned, the years rolled by,
It seems like only yesterday,
When we were young, and we would play,
The games that only children know,
Go to the places children go,
Had secret gangs, and secret dens,
Where we would go with secret friends,
Have secret passwords no one knew,
Except our gang, the secret few.
It seemed the sun would always shine,
I felt the future was all mine,
But now the future is today,
All those tomorrows rushed away,
I can't believe the years I've known,
As in the mirror, old I've grown.
With age came knowledge, wisdom too,
Suppose I've learnt a thing or two,
I've learnt that life is sometimes sad,
I've learnt that people, good and bad,
With luck grow old, as I have done,
And will look back, at childhood fun,
With some regret, a tear, maybe,
Thinking of things that used to be,
Maybe, we think what might have been,
Or might have done, or might have seen.
Then think again of childhood dreams,
Of childhood games, and childhood schemes,
As time rolled by my dreams came true,
I hope that yours, came true for you.

Jim Sargant

MY COLLIE DOG

Look at my beautiful collie dog
He is always by my side even
When I get changed to go outside
He always comes along thinking he is going for a ride.

Look at my beautiful collie dog
Looking full of fun
For we have just got back from a sheepdog trial
Where he thinks that he has won
But little does he know that soon he will be a dad
For soon there will be some puppies
The first ones I think that he has ever had.

Look at my beautiful collie dog
He knows that it is time for bed
But he will never settle down until
He has had a quick look around the yard
To make sure everything is fed.

Keith L Powell

HIDING YOUR FEELINGS

You loved when I read you poems
You said that with poetry I had a natural flair
I told you they were Shakespeare's
You said you didn't care.

When I told you of the art I loved
Of Van Gogh, Munch and Dali
How I described those prints in detail to you
I shall never forget the look in your eyes.

You said you loved my zest
For all the things I loved
It made things come alive you said
That otherwise you'd never have known.

You know me better than I know myself
You know when I'm zestful or sad
Yet I often wonder if you realise
The look in my eyes when you hold my hand.

You'll never know how I've seen you
How your smile brightens up my day
You'll never know the feelings I hide from you
Because I'm too shy to say.

I wonder if you ever realise
That beyond your blindness I see a person who is great
But you tend to use that as a barrier
And see yourself merely as additional weight.

I want to tell you so many things
How I love the curls in your hair when they fall in your eyes
I want to tell you the love I hide
That could reach from here to the skies.

The day they told me 'He's gone'
I realised I was left in a situation
Where I shall always think of what could have been
Why do people wait until it is too late?

Samantha Bailie

FIRST PAST THE POST

The Mumbo Jumbo Missing Link Band,
lived in a place called Jolly Riddle Land.

Here was the springboard from which sprang man,
so springboard valley is where the race began.

Under starters orders, on your marks, get set,
who'll be the winner is anyone's bet.

The starting pistol rang out with a blast,
and human beings were spreading fast.

It took thousands of years to cover the earth,
but who is back first to the place of birth?

The winner was the one most clever and brave,
who captured his parents and made them slave.

Glenn Granter

REMEMBER

You may in future times anon
Behold my face in a crowd
You may heed the smile is dim upon
My face, its former radiance avowed
The glowing of my happy heart
My smile that once lit up your world
Ere you shot your faithless dart
Remember as my sleepy eyes unfurled
Their love light shone alone for you
Remember that I always tried
To honour you with love so true
Remember my pain, how I cried
In despair, I, with your deceit endowed
Remember nought . . . but a face in the crowd.

Iris Kruk

INTERNET

Surfing on a wave on information,
Shopping the easy way,
Finding out what's happening on the net,
And collecting history and magazines.

Watching the computer do many tricks,
Looking at the mouse beside a cup of tea,
Waiting for the printer,
And saying, 'Wow, what new technology.'

Kenneth Mood

THE SENT VALENTINE

Scratched words that give out messages of commitment
For we remain juniors of circumstance
Party animals
Down to love and the sent valentine
Secure to the bond of loving
To that healing process of the mind
To a joining factor called love.

Roger Thornton

No Looking Back

Please look forward, don't look back
You can smile, your face won't crack.
See tomorrow not yesterday
Think of only nice things to say.
Look to the future not the past
Don't you worry, the world will last.
Forget that what has gone, see what is to come
Give love to your children just like your mum.

Don't look at last week, hold on to today
Be happy at work, rest and play.
You can forget all that has been
Look at the fields all nice and green.
You can't hold on things that have gone
Or repair the things you have done wrong.
Just you behold the things that will be
And then love and freedom you'll *see.*

Colin Allsop

IRREFUTABLE IMAGE

When the beggarman himself debases
bending from the waist
in desperate haste,
clutching at coins in conspicuous places,
who can ascertain his greatness of need?
Does he swallow pride,
or suffer inside,
a creature possessed by egoist's greed?
In a way we are all as lost as he
but tables are turned
and new lessons learned;
should we not pray, permit ourselves to see
that good is never a slave to our souls
with arms extended
all sin transcended,
obediently gratifying goals?
Obsequiousness is a last resort -
God is innate might
and He does not fight
nor fawn, 'tis not what early prophet taught.
Yet faith is concept straggler can't afford.
Beauty - artists' fad,
still makes sceptics glad,
they take it as their right, ignore the Lord
as intangible as natural sheen,
whose powers unique
are neither oblique
nor dead but great as they've ever been.

Ruth Daviat

SANDY BRIDGE

Sandy Bridge over Dean Brook
its feet stretching across this humble flow
its arms projecting into the tall trees
as if flinging them in worship and praise
to the God of creation.

Robert D Shooter

SPIRITUALITY AND SENSUALITY

It is possible for someone
to have been both
spiritual and sensual
since the age of five;
such a person uses the
spirit to control the
flesh, which is not only
weak but sometimes wild.

Compare such a life to
a horse-drawn carriage;
the horses symbolise the flesh;
the reins: the willing spirit;
the driver is the soul, the self,
the carriage: genes and environment;
the passengers are those one meets
in life; one's life affects others.

K K Kempt

WESTON-SUPER-NOWHERE

The fires have gone out
What will you do now?
Your star is falling
Can you write a new role
And rewrite your history?
The answer remains a mystery.

The world is your oyster
But you are a tainted pearl
Soiled goods get left on the shelf
Glitter soon loses its sparkle
Can you reinvent yourself again?
The answer is hiding in the rain.

You swim against the tide
Waves of words rising high
Drowning the good you have done
The tides in the affairs of one man
You could always write another book
When the fish gets free from the hook.

But you will resurface somewhere
You could always go and live
In Weston-Super-Nowhere
Away from the spotlight's glare
To peddle your new wares
No hawkers and no circulars.

The bow is bent and drawn
You shoot your arrows over the house
And hurt your brother.

Ian Barton

A Female Demand

What do women want? I ask,
Would I suborn a thankless task,
Argument, would never lie,
Like red roses, never die,
Astonish me, amaze me please,
Of things I can't, a being cease,
To live as man of male's refrain,
From you! Ruled by the twain,
Heart and mind, emotions strong,
Passions rule, so we are wrong,
Not logic cold, if you could see,
Mere sanity of reasoned be,
Give to me my finest rose,
Give to me the one who knows,
Who will tell me, I am wrong,
The lady loves, I fight so strong,
Passions, feelings, is it right?
For everything, I will fight,
The coward, bully, I will kill,
Be easy now, my love to will,
Nothing's said and nothing's sold,
A virgin left; for me the gold.

C Thornton

OH MOTHER OF MINE

A natural native kind is she charming
Sweet and kind of heart
Whose nature is so divine to me
Bright threads she weaves from a heavenly heart
Enchanting love which unfolds of one harmonious soul

Supreme is my queen of life behold as a gem of fortune
Pure and blessed how ever she can be hurt
So treat her gentle because she's quiet and not rough at heart

Oh mother of mine you are a delight, a blossom of enlightenment
As to other people you meet and judge a person as I hope they judge
You when you meet them in the street

A gentle spirit most sweet with uplifted eyes with a glaze
Like a diamond which finds her mortal bliss that we will miss.

Gary Bullock

A Day In The Park

The ground is dull cold,
I feel it against me as I lay.
My eye level is filled,
Dancing leaves pirouette in the wind.
Each has its own steps in the dance,
All are individuals, separate.

The peace is broken.
A mother passes by,
Trailing her fat person pups.
They reach to me,
Pulling and poking.
I hold my bite inside.
The tension releases a warning
It passes my lips,
Showing a glimpse of the underlip
And dagger sharp teeth.
The pups run.

The day passes gently.
People bustle beneath the grey sky.
They pass my little world.
I do not care.

The sky grows gradually black,
Water floods down.
Translucent crystals balance on my eyelashes.
Natural drums tapping
Beating with the earth rhythm.
I am dragged to my feet,
As my master and I run
Towards the shelter of home.

Clare Smith

NATURAL TONES

I am
The springtime of leaves
And song of burnt meadows
Where the winter warms
The earth's ploughed scars
Mingling with moon's soft crust.

Capricious images
Nurseling plunders
Shrouded to announce
To the world at large
Their blunders
And crystallisation
Of amorphous mass
Of feelings and sensations
Into significant forms
In a universe of values
Echoes of an inner stance.

I am
The spring sap
Of leaves
And songs of meadows
Briefs
Scars of earth
Peeled and ploughed
With bloods of
Moon's dried crust.

I am the visibility of the day
I am the invisibility of the night
I am the spring sap of the leaves
And the echoes of winter's last rites.

Durlabh Singh

IMAGINE

Daylight, slowly merging into night,
Gentle velvet, cooling, entwining with starlight,
Silvery clouds, riding on a solar stream,
Change hues, from blue, gold, red, then cream.

A gentle breeze, warm on exposed skin,
Gives peace of mind, deep from within,
Leaves stirring slowly, whisper into the dusk,
Flora's haunting, fragrant lingering musk.

Ancient constellations, twinkle into sight,
The squeak of a bat, in silent flight,
Constant buzz, from mosquito wings,
All these sensations, a summer evening brings.

Courting couples, walking slowly, fingers entwined,
Saying anything that suddenly comes to mind,
The startled chatter, from a roosting thrush,
Disturbed by a foraging hedgehog, in the under brush.

In the distance, a yellow glow, lit the sky,
The soft murmur, of traffic passing quickly by,
Rhythmic tinkle, of identification tag on chain,
As dog and companion, walked slowly down the lane.

A sense of wonder, that time stands still,
Gazing at the moon, from the top of a hill,
Its cold light, washes over the planet,
Controlling tides, of the oceans that span it.

Robert Thompson

THE FURY OF THE SEA

As the wind whips the sea up in rage,
The waves come rolling and pounding in.
Ripping at the man-made sea defences,
In its fury, determined nature will win!

While planton froths in the eruption,
Seaweed has surfaced, life in the depths past.
The sea bottom's being raked and torn apart.
Will man's sea defences still stand fast?

As its sheer force thuds against the surface,
Sending showers of water high into the air,
Cascading back on the oncoming waves,
Causing confusion in its moment of despair!

Air saturated with this sticky mist, while the
Sea hides destruction plus a magnitude of sins.
There's nothing dare ride on these waters,
The sea's anger and determination knows it wins.

Sea creatures buried safely in its depths,
Wait until its rage and fury subsides.
Man's rubbish, wood, metal, oil etc, thrown back,
How dare *they* destroy this earth's paradise!

Ann Beard

Everyday's Extinction

I want to write this poem
To try to make you see
All the problems of the world
To see that they are real
I will tell you of the pollution
That we pour into our seas
No more forest left
We have chopped down all the trees
Elephants are fewer
The whales are even less
Everyday's extinction
Until there's nothing left

Alan Green

KNOWS NO BOUNDS

Our planet's beauty knows no bounds
Such are our words
All of Mother Nature's sweet side seen
Of flowers, trees and birds

But true too, is seen her dark side
Of snails, wasps, slugs.
Weeds and breeds, mosquitoes, bees, ants, roach
And many other bugs

Is it we want to seem grateful
To God's supplies
For all the endless beauty conjured
And seen before our eyes

Does He see us as so naive
As to view but good
He does grow a natural world but
Does not make *us* of wood

We don't like nature's ugly side
He has reason
To appreciate the good there's to be some bad
For us in life's seasons

The rains, snows, frosts and gales all do
Saturate grounds
Be ye not blind for Mother Nature's
Old black side knows no bounds.

Barbara Sherlow

Empty Fields

The fields are empty now.
Silent in the sunlight,
The wheat and barley
Grow without the oversight of man.
Or so it seems to travellers
In this quiet Suffolk land.

I saw them once,
The horses;
Breasting a rise
At the headland next to the road.
In the fifties, it was,
The last time I saw the team,
The ploughman stopping them,
Talking to my friend.

He had this notion that all was ending.
Everything that he and I had known
Not so long ago, when we were boys.

Milk dipped from the churn,
Weary horses ambling home,
Saturdays in the garden,
The wheelbarrow full from the black earth,
Fecund beyond today's imagining.

And he was right.
Almost everything has gone
Except the fields themselves.
The ploughs, the drills,
The gathering of the crops still go on.
But now, what sights and sounds
Living in our memories
Are lost forever.

Richard Maslen

WOUNDS TO HEAL

We live in a wounded land
Scarred by countless years
Endless digging hands
Pounding machines
Moving ever closer to the heart
Of this earth clad in beauty
That suffers under our barrage or destruction
The seduction of greed taking us further
As we kill and plunder
Tear and poison nature's innocence
With our innocence lost
So long ago
In the garden that is dying
To become a barren land
Unless we heed the calls
The whispering in the leaves of trees
Upon the wind and in the roar of waves
Asking for us to end our pillaging
Before the heart of the land is broken
Asking that we find harmony with the world
Bringing tranquillity to the garden once more.

Edwin Page

A New World?

A new era is dawning
A new time has come
People have started mourning
For the destruction we have done.

A forest of trees is no more -
The wildlife all destroyed,
Man has defied nature's law
And life has become quickly void.

A wealth of love is no more -
Violence and murder rule,
Wrecking Mother Earth - what is it for?
Using power and wealth as a tool.

Basic human decency is no more -
Nature's anguished cries are not heard,
A lack of caring is at the core
Of this once untouched, beautiful world.

Nishani Balendra

CHANGES OF TIME, THROUGH TIMES WE LIVE

Through times I sit alone the things that go on,
I see, we see, I feel, you feel, we don't, I don't, that
Things, how knows, everyday things, time, seasons,
Changes of time, that come and go, like life itself in a
Way I guess it just goes on, it's there, it happens, it's doing it now.
Like the wind that blows, like the stars at night, to the moon so bright,
It's like a cold night time sun. Like the oceans so wide, waves to the
Beaches of white horses do ride to sandcastles in the sand.
Like the sky so blue, to the clouds that float and carry the breeze on
That endless journey, to the deepest of space we see at night, how
Far does it go of endless darkness, to the stars far and wide.
Like the rumble of thunder, so far but so near, like the
                                          blackest of clouds
Do come the lightning, that brilliant bright light that forks the sky.
Like the rain to come, as do follow the rainbow of colours that stretch
From one to one, and of the sun to shine through the days we live.

Craig Alan Hornby

PLANET EARTH: DON'T DESTROY IT

We must now begin, before it's too late
To look after our earth
Stop polluting the planet
You can help, yes you
You can use recycled materials
You can recycle yourself
We must stop the destruction of rainforests
Help wildlife habitats
Wildlife has been on earth for as long as us
It's their environment too
Don't destroy it for them
Don't destroy it for the human race
If you can help in any way, do so
Yes, you, you can help
Our earth, our planet
It's for us all, all races and creatures
Look after our planet earth
Do your part, do your bit
The earth is our future
The earth needs to be looked after
So that our children will have
A decent earth environment in the future
Not just our children but the children
Of the future
Let's not destroy before they are born
The earth is the future
Look after our earth, our planet
Planet earth, don't destroy it.

David J Hall

ANCHOR BOOKS SUBMISSIONS INVITED
SOMETHING FOR EVERYONE

ANCHOR BOOKS GEN - Any subject, light-hearted clean fun, nothing unprintable please.

THE OPPOSITE SEX - Have your say on the opposite gender. Do they drive you mad or can we co-exist in harmony?

THE NATURAL WORLD - Are we destroying the world around us? What should we do to preserve the beauty and the future of our planet - you decide!

All poems no longer than 30 lines.
Always welcome! No fee!
Plus cash prizes to be won!

Mark your envelope (eg *The Natural World*)
And send to:
Anchor Books
Remus House, Coltsfoot Drive
Woodston, Peterborough, PE2 9JX

OVER £10,000 IN POETRY PRIZES TO BE WON!

Send an SAE for details on our New Year 2000 competition!